Let's Play!

Games for Girls

Ages 5–11

Girl Scouts of the USA
420 Fifth Avenue
New York, NY 10018-2798
www.girlscouts.org

Girl Scouts®
Where Girls Grow Strong℠

Chair, National Board of Directors
Cynthia B. Thompson

National Chief Executive Officer
Kathy Cloninger

Senior Vice President, Program, Membership and Research
Sharon Hussey

Senior Director, Research and Program
Harriet Mosatche, Ph.D.

Project Manager
Verna Simpkins

Authors
Toni Eubanks, Janet Lombardi

Contributors
Debra Allen, Kathleen Cullinan, Helen Orloff, Shari Teresi

Spanish Translation
Margarita Magner

Designed by
The Harquin Group
  Illustration by Angela Martini

Inquiries related to *Let's Play! Games for Girls Ages 5–11* should be directed to Girl Scouts of the USA, 420 Fifth Avenue, 15th Floor, New York, NY 10018–2798.

For more information about Girl Scouts, visit **www.girlscouts.org.**

ISBN 0-88441-691-7
10 9 8 7 6 5 4

Library of Congress Cataloging-in-Publication Data in application.

Table of Contents

Introduction

Group play is of tremendous value to a child's development—offering fun-filled ways to build confidence, enhance skills, and nurture a healthy exploration of the outdoors. Playing games teaches girls to work on a team, take turns, problem-solve, and treat each other with respect.

In addition, games convey cultural and social values, giving girls opportunities to see how similar they and their play are to those of different ethnicities and cultural backgrounds. Games set the stage for making friends as girls interact spontaneously and discover common interests.

The games in this book are referenced by age-appropriateness, objective, number of players, materials needed, and easy-to-follow instructions. Many of the games include suggestions for variations.

For Girls with Disabilities

Though the games in *Let's Play!* have been selected to meet the needs of all girls, some girls with disabilities may require activity adaptations. Adjustments can be made as needed. A conversation with the girl and her parents/guardians can provide guidance on how to best tailor an activity to ensure full participation.

Local Girl Scout councils, as well as hospitals, mental health centers, libraries, and the Internet, are also valuable sources for information about adapting games for girls with disabilities. For a list of organizations, agencies, and associations that may be able to help with adaptations, visit the Girl Scout Website, www.girlscouts.org.

About Safety

Always keep first-aid supplies at hand and be sure to consult *Safety-Wise* (published by Girl Scouts of the USA, 2000) for safety guidelines and Program Standards before playing the games. Although many of the games contained in *Let's Play!* are not mentioned by name in *Safety-Wise*, general activity checkpoints may still apply. Lastly, become knowledgeable about any safety guidelines your council might observe.

Ready? Let's play!

Mix & Mingle Games

Mix & Mingle games are a great way for girls to get to know each other. Whether already friends or meeting for the first time, these games can help girls expand their social skills, assume a leadership role, learn something about themselves, and recognize similarities and differences within a diverse group of people.

Mix & Mingle games are useful at large-scale events where girls can expand their friendship circles.

Use Mix & Mingle games:

* At the beginning of a membership year
* At rededication ceremonies
* At inter-group ceremonies
* When a new girl joins the group

Let's Shop!

Age Group: 6-11
How Many Can Play: 4 or more
Objective: To help players become acquainted.

Materials: None

My name is Melina and I'm buying marshmallows!

How To Play

1. Gather players in a circle. Explain that they are going to a food store to buy an item that begins with the first letter of their name.

2. The first player might say, "My name is Melina and I'm buying marshmallows."

3. The second player repeats the previous player's purchase and adds one item, beginning with the first initial of her name. For example, "My name is Sasha and I am buying marshmallows and strawberries." Player three might say, "My name is Brigitte and I am buying marshmallows, strawberries, and bananas."

4. If a player misses an item or recites the items out of order, she is out of the game. The last player remaining wins.

Keep In Mind

If the group is small, have each girl buy two or more items that begin with the first letter of her name.

Centipedes

Age Group: **5-11**
How Many Can Play: **6 or more**
Objective: To be the first centipede to reach the finish line.

Materials

* ✳ A carpeted or grassy area
* ✳ Chalk or masking tape

Before You Play

Mark the start and finish lines. Designate one player to give the signal to start the game.

How To Play

1. Divide players into even teams.

2. Players kneel in single file, holding the ankles of the player directly in front. Each team is now a "centipede."

3. At the signal, centipedes move toward the finish line while on their knees.

4. If the centipede breaks, the team goes back to the starting line. The first centipede to reach the finish line is the winner.

Bubble Fun

Age Group: 5-11
How Many Can Play: 4 or more
Objective: To create the most unusual soap bubbles.

Materials

✻ Water, dishwashing liquid, and glycerin for the bubble solution (see recipe below)

✻ Plastic containers to hold the bubble solution (one for each team)

✻ Different tools for making bubbles: large bubble wands; pipe cleaners bent into shapes; plastic open fruit baskets, such as those that hold strawberries

✻ Paper towels

✻ Newspapers or towels to cover table surfaces

Before You Play

Prepare the bubble solution.

Bubble Solution
1 gallon water
1 cup dishwashing liquid
1/8 cup glycerin

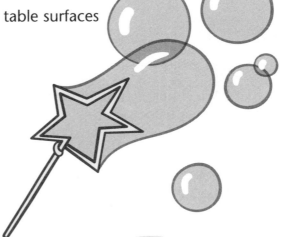

How To Play

1. Divide players into "bubble teams." Give each team the bubble-making tools.

2. Teams experiment by making bubbles in an assortment of shapes and sizes, noting their colors and patterns.

3. Teams demonstrate how to make a bubble using their favorite bubble-making tool.

4. Shuffle the teams and begin again.

Keep In Mind

Remind players not to put their mouths on the bubble wands or ingest the bubble solution. It is safest to wave the bubble-making tool in the air.

Variation

Teams can compete to see who creates the largest or the longest-lasting bubble.

Thumbnail Sketch

Age Group: 5-11
How Many Can Play: 4 or more
Objective: To help players become acquainted.

Materials

* Timer

How To Play

1. Each girl chooses a partner.

2. Designate a timekeeper.

3. Within 3 minutes (or less), players try to learn five things about their partner by asking and answering questions such as, What is your name? Where do you live? What do you like best about Girl Scouts? Do you have a pet? What is the most fun thing you have done today?

4. When the timer sounds, players take turns presenting their thumbnail sketches. Try them in American Sign Language.

What's your favorite?

Tap your middle finger on your chin.

(your + favorite + what?)

Speller's Spider Web

Age Group: 6-11
How Many Can Play: 4 or more
Objective: To form as many words as possible by connecting letters within the spider web.

Materials

* Paper * Markers and pencils
* Timer

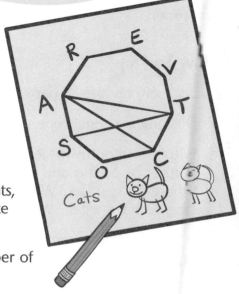

Before You Play

1. Divide players into even teams.

2. Draw large, octagon-shaped spelling webs; one for each team. At each of the octagon's eight points, write one letter of the alphabet. Include appropriate vowels and consonants to form simple words.

3. Make enough copies of each web for the number of teams and rounds you intend to play.

4. Set a time limit for each round. Designate a timekeeper.

How To Play

1. Divide players into pairs. Designate one player as the scribe.

2. Give each pair a copy of the same spider web.

3. Start the timer and say "Go."

4. Players find words by drawing lines, in any direction, from one letter to another. Players may use a letter more than once. Each time a word is formed, the scribe writes it on a list.

5. When the timer sounds, the scribe reads the list of words. The pair with the most words is the winner.

6. To play again, change partners, or pairs can work on a different spider web.

What's the Same?

Age Group: 5-11
How Many Can Play: 6 or more
Objective: To guess the team's common interest or characteristic.

Materials: None

How To Play

1. Divide players into two teams.

2. The first team quietly talks among themselves to identify something they all have in common (e.g., a favorite sport, TV show, color, book, food, or a physical characteristic, such as eye color, hair color, color of clothing, etc.).

3. The second team then asks questions, each requiring only a "Yes" or "No" answer, to try and guess the opposing team's common trait.

Variation

When each team settles on something it has in common,
players act it out while the other team tries to guess what's the same.

Line Up!

Age Group: 5-11
How Many Can Play: 6 or more
Objective: To be the first to line up in a particular order.

Materials: None

Before You Play

If the group is large, count off to divide into even teams. (Ones become a team, twos become a team, etc.) Players can remain in their groups for a second round, or count off again to form different groups.

How To Play

1. **Round one:** Players line up according to the alphabetical order of their first name, beginning with A and ending with Z (or beginning with Z and ending with A).

2. **Round two:** Players line up according to their birthdate, beginning with January 1 and ending with December 31.

3. **Round three:** Players line up in height order.

4. The team that lines up first wins.

January

February

March

Nature Scavenger Hunt

Age Group: 6-11
How Many Can Play: 4 or more
Objective: To be the first to spot all of the items
on the scavenger hunt list.

Materials

* Paper and pencils
* Timer

How To Play

1. Explain that the scavenger hunt is not to collect items, but to locate and record as many items on the list as possible within a given amount of time.

2. Designate a timekeeper. Players must return to the starting line when they hear an agreed-upon call or sound.

3. Distribute a scavenger hunt list to participants.

 THE SCAVENGER HUNT LIST COULD INCLUDE:

SOMETHING LARGE

SOMETHING SMALL

SOMETHING COLORED

(Continued on next page)

SOMETHING FRAGRANT
SOMETHING NEWLY GROWN
SOMETHING PRETTY
SOMETHING TINY
SOMETHING THAT DOES NOT BELONG IN NATURE
SOMETHING ROUND
SOMETHING SOFT
SOMETHING HARD
SOMETHING STRAIGHT
SOMETHING THAT MAKES A NOISE
SOMETHING CAMOUFLAGED
SOMETHING THAT CHANGED THE ENVIRONMENT

Keep In Mind

Players can participate in the scavenger hunt individually, in pairs, or in groups, depending on the size of the designated area. Each participant or group should be familiar with the area and know the signal for returning to the starting point. This game is designed to be played outdoors but could be modified for an indoor activity.

Variation

Use digital cameras to record items on the scavenger hunt list.

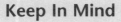

Active Games

Active games are especially good while camping, at school fields or local parks, or in a backyard. Consider active games when girls are enjoying sleepovers at the mall or have access to a gymnasium, basement, or recreation room.

Introduce active games when:

* Girls have been sitting or playing quiet games and need a change of pace

* Girls want to play team sports

* You want to introduce fitness and healthy living projects

* Girls are working toward awards, such as the Brownie Girl Scout Sports and Games Try-It or the Junior Girl Scout Swimming Badge.

Circle Ball

Age Group: 5-8
How Many Can Play: 4 or more
Objective: To kick the ball out of the circle.

Materials

* One medium-size ball

How To Play

1. One player volunteers to be "It."

2. Players stand in a circle with their feet apart. "It" stands in the center with the ball.

3. "It" tries to kick the ball out of the circle through another player's legs.

4. The other players can use only their feet to block the ball and kick it back into the center of the circle.

5. When "It" kicks the ball between another player's legs and out of the circle, she trades places with that player.

Balloon Relay

Age Group: 6-11
How Many Can Play: 4 or more
Objective: To be the first team to finish the relay.

Materials

* Water balloons (at least 3-4 for every girl and for every round)

Before You Play

1. Prepare water balloons. Players can help fill balloons.

2. Mark start and finish lines.

How To Play

1. Divide players into even teams.

2. Place a pile of water balloons at the start line for each team.

3. When "Go" is called, the first player on each team picks up a balloon and runs to the finish line.

4. At the finish line, she sits on her balloon until it pops, then runs back to the start line.

5. The next player grabs a balloon and repeats the sequence.

6. If a player's balloon pops before she reaches the finish line, she must return to the start line for a new balloon and begin again.

7. The first team to finish the relay is the winner.

Keep In Mind

This is a wet and messy game (pieces of balloon will need to be picked up at the end) and is best played outdoors with girls wearing swimsuits.

Variations

* Pairs from each team hold a water balloon between their stomachs and race to the finish line.

* Pairs from each team race with water balloons between their knees.

Grab Bag

Age Group: 5-11
How Many Can Play: 4 or more
Objective: To put on the least amount of clothing.

Materials

* A laundry bag filled with old clothes in various sizes—hats, shoes, shirts, aprons, socks, jackets, gloves, scarves, etc.

How To Play

1. Players sit in a circle. One player is selected to be the "caller."

2. Caller stands outside of the circle with her back to the group.

3. Players in the circle pass the laundry bag. When caller yells "Stop," whoever has the laundry bag pulls out an article of clothing, with eyes closed, and puts it on.

4. The game continues until the laundry bag is empty. The player wearing the fewest articles of clothing is the winner. The person wearing the most clothes is the next caller.

Keep In Mind

Laundry bag can include costume jewelry, eyeglass frames, or anything that players can easily put on.

Go, Car, Go!

Age Group: 5-8
How Many Can Play: 8 or more
Objective: To be the first "car" to return to her place in the circle.

Materials: None

Before You Play

Ask players to choose names of favorite cars and the "car problems" they might have.

How To Play

1. Players sit in a circle and count off from one to four. For example, ones are Fords, twos are Volvos, etc. Designate a "caller."

2. Before the cars begin their race, the caller announces some type of car trouble (e.g., a flat tire for the Volvos could mean those cars must hop on one foot around the circle; running out of gas could mean cars must crab-walk).

3. The cars then race each other around the circle, hampered by their specific car trouble.

4. The winners from each group then race each other around the circle.

Beanbag Bull's Eye

Age Group: 5-11
How Many Can Play: 2 or more
Objective: To toss a beanbag and score the most points.

Materials

* Poster board
* Marker and tape to draw an indoor target or chalk to draw a pavement target
* Beanbags
* Paper and pencils

Before You Play

1. Draw a large donut-shaped target. If playing indoors, draw the target on a large sheet of paper and tape it to the floor. If playing outdoors, draw the target on the pavement with chalk.

2. Mark sections large enough for a beanbag to fit inside without touching the borders.

3. Assign points, ranging from 5 to 30, for each section, with the highest value in the middle of the target.

4. Mark a starting line based on the skill level of the players.

How To Play

1. Players take turns throwing the beanbags into one of the sections. Depending on the number of players, each should get 1 to 3 throws during each round.

2. An assigned scorekeeper records a running tally of the scores.

3. Points are scored if the beanbag lands within a section without touching the borders.

4. The winner is determined by the highest score, or by the first player to reach a pre-determined number of points, such as 100.

Jump Rope Jump

Age Group: 6-11
How Many Can Play: 4 or more
Objective: To progress through the different jumps accurately and without touching the ropes.

Materials

* One 12-to 15-foot length of 1/4- to 1/2-inch-wide elastic or clothesline rope.

Before You Play

1. Tie the ends of the elastic or rope together to form a circle.

2. Designate two girls as jump rope anchors. Rotate anchors, perhaps after every three or four jumpers.

3. Players determine the sequence of jumps in and out of the elastic circle. For example:
   a. Jump in and out on one foot.
   b. Jump in and out with both feet.
   c. Jump in, clap, jump out.
   d. Jump in, turn around, jump out.

How To Play

1. Anchors face each other with the elastic stretched taut around their legs, about 6 to 8 inches from the ground.

2. Players stand single file in front of the jump rope circle.

3. Anchors call out the sequence of jumps.

4. If a player misses a jump, she goes to the end of the line. The game continues until every girl has a chance to play.

Variation

Have players create their own jump sequences.

Spot the Lion

Age Group: 5-11

How Many Can Play: 8 or more

Objective: To be the team with the most players in its corner when the game ends.

Materials

* Masking tape or self-sticking labels
* Scissors
* Pen or marker

Before You Play

1. Cut strips of masking tape or have labels for each player. Write "lion" on only one strip or label; leave the rest blank.

2. Designate a game leader.

How To Play

1. Divide players into even teams. Assign teams to their own corner or place.

2. On the leader's signal, players scatter. Then, they stand with their eyes shut while the game leader runs to each player and presses a strip of tape on her back.

3. When everyone has been labeled (including one player as lion), the leader shouts, "The lion is loose!"

4. Players open their eyes and run around trying to spot the lion. When one player spots the lion, she hurries to her team spot, trying not to arouse the lion's suspicion. The longer the lion goes unidentified, the greater number of players will make it back to their corner.

5. If a player suspects that she is the lion, she goes to the center of the room and roars loudly. When she roars, all players freeze.

6. If the girl who roared is the lion, the game is over. If the girl who roared is not the lion, the game continues for one more minute.

7. The winning team has the most players in its corner when the game ends.

Hopscotch Relay

Age Group: 5-8
How Many Can Play: 2 or more
Objective: To be the first to draw a complete stick figure inside a hopscotch square.

Materials

* Markers for each player (stones, coins, or buttons)

* Colored chalk

Before You Play

Draw a rectangle (approximately 3 ft x 8 ft) with chalk on the sidewalk, as shown. Divide the rectangle into 10 equal spaces.

How To Play

1. The first player tosses her marker into a square. If it lands on a line or outside the hopscotch grid, the player picks it up and waits for her next turn.

2. When a marker lands inside one of the 10 spaces, the player hops through the hopscotch squares.

3. When she hops through successfully, by not missing a square or stepping on a line, she begins drawing her stick figure in the square where her marker landed. (It takes a minimum of six good tosses to complete one stick figure drawing—a circle for the head, a line for the body, two

lines for the arms, two lines for the legs.) (Players can use different colors to identify their drawings or initial them.)

4. On subsequent turns, player must toss her marker in the same section and hop through successfully to add to the drawing. If her marker lands in a different space and she hops through the grid, she begins a new drawing.

5. The first player to draw a complete figure is the winner.

Rattlesnake Hopscotch

Age Group: 5-8
How Many Can Play: 2 or more
Objective: To take ownership of the most hopscotch squares.

Materials

* Chalk

Before You Play

Draw 10 or more connected circles, each approximately 1 foot in diameter, in a serpentine shape. Since the player who goes first has an advantage, draw numbers to establish order of participation.

How To Play

1. The first player begins at one end of the snake and hops from circle to circle to the end. If she lands on a line, or outside of the snake, she has to begin again. After a player reaches the end, she writes her initials (or a symbol) inside any circle of her choice. The other players cannot land in that circle; they must jump over it.

2. On subsequent turns, players can land on their own initialed circles with both feet.

3. Players continue to initial circles of their choice as they successfully hop through the trail.

4. Play continues until all of the circles are initialed, or until one player captures the most circles. The player with the most initialed circles at the end of the game is the winner.

Keep In Mind

1. It is best to have no more than three players for each hopscotch trail.

2. A good strategy for players is to initial two squares in a row, making it harder for opponents.

Variations

❋ On the first turn, allow each player two chances to hop from beginning to end.

❋ For younger girls, or for girls who are physically challenged:

Shorten the "snake."

Hop twice in each circle, perhaps switching legs.

Jump with both feet or step across the circles.

Rest once or twice on the way through the snake.

Girl Scout Hopscotch

Age Group: 5-8
How Many Can Play: 2 or more
Objective: To be the first to complete the hopscotch.

Materials

❋ Chalk

❋ Markers for each player (stones, coins, or buttons)

Before You Play

1. Draw a rectangle (approximately 3 ft x 8 ft). Divide the rectangle into 10 spaces. Draw a half circle at the top. With more than three or four players, divide the group into even teams and create one hopscotch field per team.

2. Write the words of the Girl Scout Law within each square.

(Continued on next page)

3. Designate a starting line, with distance determined by the players' ages and abilities.

How To Play

1. From behind the starting line, the first player aims her marker for the first square, "Honest and Fair."

2. If the marker lands in the "Honest and Fair" square, she hops over that square, and all the way through the hopscotch field. If she makes it through the field (turning around at the top), on the return trip she picks up her marker from the first square. On her next turn, she aims for the next square, "Friendly and Helpful."

3. If a player misses her toss, steps on a line, or lands with two feet, her turn ends. On her next turn, she begins with the square where she left off. (She does not need to start from the beginning.) The winner is the first player to go through the hopscotch field successfully.

Variations

* Allow younger or physically challenged players to hop with two feet.

* Use a buddy system—one girl tosses and another girl hops.

* Write the Girl Scout Law in Spanish.

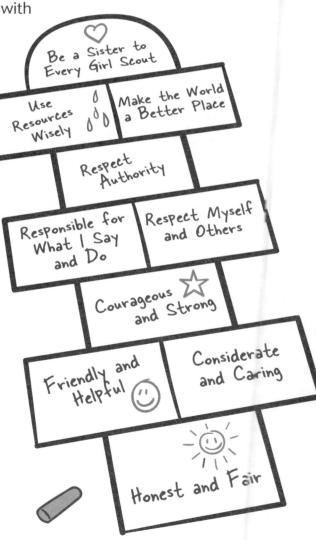

Team-Building Games

Team-building games require cooperation between players to reach a common goal and are designed to strengthen group unity through play.

Use team-building games to:

* Build on an already-established strong group dynamic

* Strengthen group unity

* Minimize exclusive, cliquish behavior

* Work together toward a common goal

Chase the Tail

Age Group: 5-11
How Many Can Play: 6 or more
Objective: To work as a team to grab the opponent's tail.

Materials

* Colorful bandanas (one for each team)

How To Play

1. Divide players into two even teams. Have each team form a single line.

2. Place the "tail" (bandana) in the pocket or waistband of the last girl in each line.

3. Players hold the waist of the girl standing directly in front of them and cannot let go during the chase.

4. On a signal, the leader of each line begins to chase the other team's tail. Only the leader can grab the other team's tail.

5. Once the tail of either team is grabbed, change leaders and start the game again.

Car and Driver

Age Group: 5-8
How Many Can Play: 6 or more
Objective: To navigate your "car" through an obstacle course.

Materials

* Items for obstacle course: chairs, cones, boxes, a tower of blocks, etc.
* Blindfolds (bandanas)
* Chalk or masking tape

Before You Play

Designate start and finish lines. Set up the obstacle course, leaving enough room for players to navigate through.

How To Play

1. Divide players into pairs with one designated as the "driver" and the other as the "car."

2. The driver stands behind the car with her hands on the car's shoulders. The car is blindfolded.

3. The car can only go where her driver steers her. No one may speak!

4. The driver must steer her car safely around the obstacles.

5. Once a pair reaches the finish line, they exchange places and play again. The game is over when everyone has driven through the obstacle course.

Variation

Pairs can all drive at the same time with a staggered obstacle course. The pair that makes it through the obstacle course first, without any accidents, is the winner.

Caterpillar Race

Age Group: 6-11
How Many Can Play: 6 or more
Objective: To be the first team to finish the race.

Materials: None

How To Play

1. Divide players into even teams and have each team form a single line. Designate someone to shout "Go."

2. Players stand with their feet apart and hold the shoulders of the girl directly in front of them.

3. At the signal, the last girl in line drops to her hands and knees and crawls through the legs of the girls on her team.

4. When she gets to the front, she jumps up and becomes the first girl in the line.

5. The player behind her grabs her shoulders, and the girl who is now last in line crawls through to become the head of the line.

6. Players repeat the sequence until every girl has made it to the front of the line.

Variations

* Teams can race to a designated finish line.

* After the last girl becomes the first in the line, players can turn around and crawl back.

Book Worm

Age Group: 5-11
How Many Can Play: 6 or more
Objective: To be the first team to make it to the finish line.

Materials

* A book for each player
* Chalk or masking tape

Before You Play

Mark start and finish lines.

How To Play

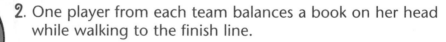

1. Divide players into even teams.

2. One player from each team balances a book on her head while walking to the finish line.

3. If a player drops her book, she is frozen.

4. The next team member, while balancing a book on her head, picks up the fallen book and hands it to the frozen player. If her book drops, both players are frozen and must wait for next teammate to unfreeze them by picking up two books.

5. The first team to get all of their players to the finish line is the winner.

Variations

* Add obstacles between the start and finish lines.

* Hold hands with a partner.

Human Spelling Bee

Age Group: 5-11

How Many Can Play: 8 or more

Objective: To use bodies to form letters or words.

Materials

* Paper and pencils
* Bowl
* Timer (optional)

Before You Play

Write letters that are easy to shape (e.g., A, E, F, H, I) and simple words (e.g., BET, HAT, GIRL, etc.) on slips of paper, fold, and place in bowl.

How To Play

1. Divide players into even teams.

2. In turn, each team chooses a paper from the bowl.

3. Players arrange themselves into the shape of letters to spell words. Teams guess the words or letters the other team has formed.

Keep In Mind

Use simpler words for smaller groups and younger girls.

Variation

Set a timer to see which team can form words and/or letters fastest.

Number Volley

Age group: 6-11
How Many Can Play: 4 or more
Objective: To keep the ball in the air as long as possible.

Materials

* Beach balls or foam balls (one for every four players)

How To Play

1. Divide players into even teams. Each team forms a circle and players count off according to how many are on each team. For example, if four players are on a team, count from 1 to 4.

2. Player one begins by throwing the ball straight up into the air and calling out "two." Player two then hits the ball and calls out "three."

3. Players continue in number order without letting the ball touch the ground.

4. If the ball touches the ground or is hit out of order, the team receives one point and begins again.

5. The team with the fewest points is the winner.

Two!

Variation

If there is only one team, players can see how many rounds they can go *without* scoring.

Loop the Hoop

Age Group: 5-11
How Many Can Play: 4 or more
Objective: To move the hoop from player to player without letting go of hands.

Materials

* One or more hula hoops (depends on size of group)

How To Play

1. Players stand in a circle, holding hands.

2. Hang a hula hoop over one player.

3. While holding hands, players pass the hoop completely around the circle without it hitting the ground.

Variations

* For a large group, use two hoops, starting side-by-side, but going in different directions. The game ends when the two hula hoops meet.

* Divide players into even teams and see which team finishes first.

Pass the Ball, Please

Age Group: 6-11
How Many Can Play: 5 or more
Objective: To pass a ball from one end of a line to the other end without using hands or letting the ball touch the ground.

Materials

❋ A ball (the smaller the ball, the more difficult; the larger the ball, the easier)

How To Play

1. Players sit on the floor in a line with their legs straight out.

2. The ball is placed between the ankles of the first girl who, without touching it, passes it to the next girl.

3. If the ball touches the ground, the team must begin again.

Variations

❋ Teams can race against each other. Once the ball reaches the end of the line, it can be passed back to the front.

❋ Add more balls or have balls traveling in both directions.

Shoe Relay

Age Group: 8-11
How Many Can Play: 8 or more
Objective: To be the first team to complete the relay.

Materials

* Players' shoes
* Chalk or masking tape

Before You Play

1. Mark a start line. Have players remove their shoes and place in a pile away from the start line.

2. Explain that time should not be wasted searching for a shoe that fits (a too-small shoe can be worn on the front of the foot) and that players may not choose their own shoes.

3. Make sure players have enough room to maneuver and the game is conducted at a calm pace.

How To Play

1. Divide players into even teams and gather at the start line. On a signal, the first player from each team runs to the pile, grabs one shoe, puts it on her foot, and runs back to her team.

2. Once back with her team, she removes the shoe and hands it to the next player. The next player then runs to the pile (carrying the shoe), throws it on the pile, and selects a different shoe to wear.

3. When the last player returns the shoe to the pile, she runs back to her team.

4. The first team to have every player wear and return a shoe is the winner.

Variation

To make this game more challenging, have players grab two different shoes from the pile, put them on, and run back to their team.

Quiet Games

 Quiet games can help focus girls' attention and provide a transition between activities. They are good choices when:

✳ Girls need to settle down after a physical activity

✳ Girls have different arrival times at a meeting place

✳ Girls need a transitional activity before beginning something new

Alphabet

Age Group: 6-11
How Many Can Play: 2 or more
Objective: Create the most words beginning with an assigned letter.

Materials

* Paper and pencils
* Timer

Before You Play

Designate a timekeeper and "caller."
Set a time limit for each round.

How To Play

1. Divide players into even teams.
   Choose one player from each team
   to record the words.

2. The caller announces a letter of her
   choice (callers do not have to proceed
   in alphabetical order), sets the timer,
   and gives the signal to begin.

3. Players think of as many words as
   possible that begin with that letter.

4. When time is up, teams compare lists. The team with the most words wins.

Variations

* Only accept words with four or more letters, or only certain parts of speech,
  such as nouns or verbs.

* Call out only difficult letters, such as "Q" and "Z."

Alphabet Story

Age Group: 6-11
How Many Can Play: 4 or more
Objective: To create a group story using designated
letters of the alphabet.

Materials: None

How To Play

1. Choose a player to describe a situation (e.g., a fire, a hike in the woods, the first day of school, etc.).

2. The first player begins the story with a sentence that starts with the letter "A." For example, "At 12:00, Rona rushed to the window." (Second player: "Black smoke filled the sky above the playground." Third player: "Cars were stopping on the highway.")

3. The game is over when the stories end logically or the group has gone through the alphabet as far as possible.

Black smoke filled the sky above the playground!

Kim's Game

Kim's Game is based on a story by Rudyard Kipling. In the story, Kim becomes friends with a jeweler who teaches him to increase his powers of observation by studying a tray full of jewels. Kim's Game appears in the first handbook for Girl Scouts, *How Girls Can Help Their Country*.

Age Group: 6-11
How Many Can Play: 2 or more
Objective: To observe and then recall as many items as possible.

Materials

* Table or tray

* Assortment of 12–24 small objects (e.g., buttons, coins, costume jewelry, small toys, crayons, rocks, shells, feathers, paper clips, stamps, etc.)

* Cloth large enough to cover the objects

* Timer

* Paper and pencils

Before You Play

Place objects on the tray or table and cover with the cloth. Explain that players will have 5–10 seconds to look at the objects once the cloth is removed. Designate a time-keeper who will remove and replace the cloth.

How To Play

1. Remove the cloth to reveal the objects and start the timer.

2. When the timer sounds, replace the cloth and give the players a certain amount of time to record what they recall seeing on the table or tray.

3. The player who correctly recalls the most objects is the winner.

Variation

To make this game more challenging, add more objects, shorten the viewing time, and/or require players to remember more details, such as color or shape. To make this game easier, reduce the number of objects and/or allow more viewing time.

Stop!
(A Game from Mexico)

Age Group: 8-11
How Many Can Play: 6 or more
Objective: To think of words that fit in certain categories.

Materials

* Game sheets
* Pencils
* Timer

Before You Play

Prepare game sheets. Label each column with a category (e.g., color, flower, fruit, animal, clothing, etc.) and use the last column for the total. (See page 42 for example.)

How To Play

1. One player begins by reciting the letters of the alphabet in order.

2. The player to her right says "Stop!" on any letter she chooses. This will be the letter that all players will use.

3. Players fill in the columns with words that begin with that letter within a certain time (approximately 2–3 minutes). The player who selected the letter can also be the timekeeper, saying "Stop!" when the timer sounds.

4. Players take turns reading their words in each category. Players get 10 points for each word, but if another player has the same word, they each get 5.

5. The player with the highest score is the winner.

(Continued on next page)

Game Sheet Diagram: For the letter "B":

Color	Flower	Fruit	Animal	Clothing	TOTAL
blue		banana	buffalo	blouse	
5 points	0 points	5 points	10 points	5 points	25 points

Variation

Let the girls choose different categories.

¡Alto!
(un juego de Méjico)

Edad: 8-11

Cantidad de jugadoras: 6 o más.

El objetivo: Pensar rápido e identificar palabras que correspondan a varias categorías.

Materiales

* Páginas de actividades
* Lápices
* Marcador de tiempo

Antes de comenzar el juego

Prepare las páginas de actividades por anticipado. Asígnele una categoría a cada columna (por ejemplo: color, fruta, flor, animal, ropa, total.)

Cómo jugar

1. Una de las jugadoras recita las letras del alfabeto en orden.

2. La jugadora sentada a su derecha dice "¡Alto!" al oír la letra que quiere. Esa será la letra que las todas usarán.

3. Las jugadoras entonces tienen un tiempo limitado, digamos de 2–3 minutos, para escribir palabras que comiencen con esa letra (véase el ejemplo). La jugadora que selecciona la letra es también la que marca el tiempo y dice "¡Alto!" cuando se acabe el tiempo.

4. Las jugadoras se turnan para leer sus respuestas para cada categoría. Las jugadoras reciben 10 puntos por cada palabra, pero si otra jugadora tiene la misma palabra, entonces cada una recibe 5 puntos.

5. La ganadora es aquella que tenga al final la puntuación más alta.

Diagrama: Usando la letra "B":

Color	Flor	Fruta	Animal	Ropa	TOTAL
blanco		banana	burro	blusa	
5 puntos	0 puntos	5 puntos	10 puntos	5 puntos	25 puntos

Variación

Deje que las niñas inventen diferentes categorías para usar en el juego.

Buzz

Age Group: 6-11
How Many Can Play: 2 or more
Objective: To say "Buzz" instead of a number.

Materials: None

How To Play

1. Players sit or stand in a circle. They choose a "Buzz" number that will also include the multiples of that number. For example, if the number chosen is 3, the multiples of 3 will include 6, 9, 12, 15, 18, 21, and so on.

2. Players count in turn, as quickly as possible, starting with the number 1.

3. When a player comes to a multiple of the chosen buzz number, she must say "Buzz" instead of the number.

4. If a player says "Buzz" in the wrong place or says the multiple of the number instead of "Buzz," she must go out of the circle.

5. The game continues until only one player is left.

Variations

* For younger players, use multiples of the numbers two or five (i.e., one, buzz, three, buzz, etc.).

* If a player misses, instead of remaining out for the duration of the game, allow her to re-enter when the next player misses.

* For a more challenging game, use multiples of two or more numbers.

1, 2, 3 in a Row

Age Group: 6-11
How Many Can Play: 2 or More
Objective: To turn three cards face up in numerical order.

Materials

* Deck of playing cards

How To Play

1. Shuffle the cards. Place them in rows, face down, on the floor.

2. Players take turns turning three cards face up, looking for a numerical sequence or run. Ace is low, or one. For example, a run could consist of ace, two, and three, or six, seven, and eight, regardless of suit. When players have a run, they keep those cards.

3. If a player does not turn over a run, she returns the three cards, face down in the spread, and the next player takes her turn. (It's important to remember the location and value of the cards as they are turned face up.)

4. The player with the most runs wins.

Variation

Players must make runs of three numbers in the same suit.

ꞁut the Box!

Materials

* Game boards
* Pair of dice
* Markers, such as coins or buttons
* Paper and pencils

Before You Play

Involve the girls in making the game
boards, or make them in advance (see
illustration). The play area is a grid of 12
squares, four rows of three squares each.
Number the squares from 1 to 12.

How To Play

1. Players take turns rolling the dice. The player with the lowest number goes first.

2. The first player rolls the dice and adds up her score. She may divide the total
   face value in any way to cover as many of the numbers on her board as
   possible. For example, if her total score is 4, she can cover squares 1 and 3
   or only square 4. The entire face value, however, must be used.

3. Players continue to take turns rolling the dice and covering numbers on their
   boards. If a player cannot use her entire score, she passes the dice to the
   next player. Numbers already covered cannot be recovered or uncovered.
   After numbers 7 through 12 are covered, players throw only one die.

4. The round is won by the first player to completely fill her card. Players who
   do not fill their cards are charged penalty points. For example, if a round ends
   and a player has not covered numbers 6 and 8, her penalty score is 14. After
   an agreed-upon number of rounds, the winner is the player with the
   lowest score.

Define It!

Age Group: 8-11
How Many Can Play: 2 or more
Objective: To guess the definitions of unusual words.

Materials

* Dictionary
* Paper and pencils

How To Play

1. Divide players into even teams. Designate team leaders.

2. The team leader selects a word from the dictionary and writes the definition on a slip of paper. (Short definitions are best.)

3. Team members work together to arrive at a fake definition for the word and then write it on a different strip of paper.

4. The team leader reads both definitions aloud.

5. The opposing team tries to guess which definition is correct.

6. The team that stumps the other team more frequently is the winner.

Variation

Teams must use the word in a sentence.

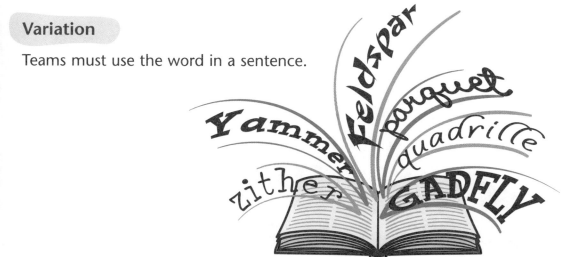

Shape Up

Age Group: 5-11

How Many Can Play: 2 or more

Objective: To replicate a design by listening to instructions.

Materials

* Colored construction paper
* Scissors
* Glue sticks
* Timer

Before You Play

1. Cut sets of shapes (circles, squares, rectangles, etc.) in various colors and sizes (small, medium, large) from construction paper. You will need identical sets for each pair of players.

2. Explain that the first player will give instructions to her partner for making a design within a time limit.

3. Designate a timekeeper.

How To Play

1. Divide players into pairs. Determine who will be the first player for each pair.

2. Give each pair of players a set of identical shapes. Players sit back-to-back so that neither can see what the other is doing.

3. The timekeeper sets the timer and says "Go."

4. Player one begins to make a design with her shapes, at the same time telling her partner where she is gluing each piece. For example: "I'm gluing the large red circle in the center. I'm gluing the small blue square over the large red circle."

5. Player two attempts to make the same design.

6. When the timer sounds, players compare how close the two designs match.

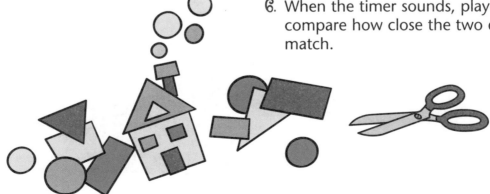

Picture This

Age Group: 6-11
How Many Can Play: 4 or more
Objective: To be the first team to guess the drawn object.

Materials

* Paper and pencils, markers, or crayons

Before You Play

A designated game leader makes a list of objects that the artists will draw.

How To Play

1. Divide players into even teams. Count off within teams to determine who goes first (i.e., ones go first, then twos, etc.). Each team is given a crayon, marker, or pencil and paper.

(Continued on next page)

2. On a starting signal, all number one players, the "artists," run to the game leader, who whispers the name of an object each artist must draw. On a second starting signal, players run back to their teams and immediately begin their drawing.

3. When team members correctly guess the object, the artist runs back to the game leader.

4. The first team to send its artist back to the game leader wins one point.

5. Number two players of each team then become the artists and the game proceeds.

6. After a designated number of rounds, the team with the most points wins.

Keep In Mind

Simple objects such as houses, cats, or trees can be used with younger players and more complex objects or concepts can be used for older players.

Variation

The game leader brings objects for the artists to touch while holding their hands behind their backs. None of the players are allowed to see the object. When the artists have felt the object, they run back to their teams and draw a picture of what they think they have felt. Team members try to guess what the object is.

Travel Games

Besides offering an antidote to the "Are we there yet?" syndrome, travel games can provide girls with an opportunity to learn about the land-scape, transportation, and each other. Travel games can fuel group spirit and anticipation for the excursion.

Enjoy travel games when:

* The group is traveling by car, bus, train, or plane

* The environment offers a good opportunity to observe something new or unusual

Alphabet Search

Age Group: 5-11
How Many Can Play: 2 or more
Objective: To find letters of the alphabet, starting with "A."

Materials: None

How To Play

1. Beginning with "A," look for letters of the alphabet. Letters can appear on anything: trucks, buildings, billboards, license plates, etc.

2. Players say the letter they find and where they found it, and then move on to the next letter of the alphabet.

3. The first player to get to the letter "Z," or the first player to find the most letters within a specific time period, is the winner.

Cliffhanger

Age Group: 5-11
How Many Can Play: 3 or more
Objective: To create a suspenseful group story.

Materials

✳ Paper and pencils (optional)

How To Play

1. One player chooses a title and begins a suspenseful story.

2. When she gets to a cliffhanger (using the words "And then. . ."), she stops and the next player continues the story.

3. The player who concludes the story can then begin another.

Variations:

✳ Tell stories that are humorous, perhaps with titles such as "The Weirdest First Day of School" or "My Crazy Neighbors."

✳ Write names of characters (from TV, books, music bands, etc.) on one slip of paper and settings on another. Girls choose characters and settings and use them as the basis for a story.

And then...

License Plates

Age Group: 6-11
How Many Can Play: 2 or more
Objective: To find license plates from different states.

Materials

* Paper and pencils
* Timer
* A United States map for each player or group (optional)

How To Play

Make a list of out-of-state license plates as they are spotted.

Variations

* See who finds the most out-of-state license plates within a time limit.

* See who finds a license plate from a state that is the farthest from your state.

* Keep a group journal of out-of-state license plates. Record the date, state, and state motto. Mark them on a map of the United States.

Lines and Dots

Age Group: 6-11
How Many Can Play: 2 or more
Objective: To complete the most squares by connecting dots.

Materials

* Paper and pencils
* Graph paper (optional)

Before You Play

Prepare a grid of dots ahead of time. (Graph paper is good for this.)

How To Play

1. Players take turns drawing a line between two dots. The lines can be horizontal or vertical (not diagonal). Lines can be drawn anywhere within the grid.

2. The object is to prevent the other player from forming a complete square. When a player completes a square, she writes her initials inside and takes another turn.

3. The player who completes the most squares is the winner.

Rock, Scissors, Paper

Age Group: 6-11
How Many Can Play: 2 or more
Objective: To choose the winning "tool."

Materials: None

How To Play

1. Divide players into pairs. Players hold one palm face up. They lay their other hand in a closed fist on top of their open palm.

2. Player pairs count to three, in unison, while hitting their fist into their palm at each count.

3. On the count of "three," they turn their fist into the "tool" of their choice: rock (a closed fist), paper (an open palm), or scissors (two fingers in a sideways V-shape).

4. The winner is determined by the choice of object. A rock can win by crushing the scissors; paper can win by covering the rock; scissors can win by cutting the paper. If players both come up with the same object, it is a draw and they go again.

Travel Bingo

Age Group: 5-11
How Many Can Play: 2 or more
Objective: To be the first player to "bingo."

Materials

* Poster board
* Ruler
* Pencil
* Pictures from magazines
* Sticky notes (1-inch squares) for bingo markers

Before You Play

Make bingo game cards ahead of time. Divide 9"x 9" cards into a grid of nine 1-inch squares. Players decorate their game cards by drawing pictures of things they might see on the trip (e.g., animals, flowers, landmarks, etc.) or by pasting pictures from magazines onto the squares.

How To Play

1. When players spot an object on their cards, they cover it with a sticky note.

2. The winner is the first player to cover three items in a row, horizontally, vertically, or diagonally.

I'm Thinking Of...

Age Group: 6-11
How Many Can Play: 3 or more
Objective: To think of an object difficult for the other players to guess.

Materials

* Paper and pencil (optional)

How To Play

1. The lead player thinks of or writes a secret word: anything that will be familiar to the other players.

2. The player to her left goes first. She must ask questions about the word that the lead player can answer with a "Yes" or "No." For example, "Is it an animal?" (This game is also known as 20 Questions or Animal, Vegetable, Mineral.)

3. The first questioner continues to ask questions as long as she receives "Yes" for an answer. A "No" answer ends her turn and the next player goes.

4. A player can only guess the secret word while it is her turn. The player who guesses the word becomes the next lead player. If no one guesses the word, the lead player goes again.

Keep In Mind

Younger girls may need help categorizing things as animal, vegetable, or mineral or person, place, or thing. To guess the secret word, players should remember the lead player's answers as they are all clues.

Make a Map

Age Group: 5-11
How Many Can Play: 1 or more
Objective: To create a picture map of a road trip.

Materials

* A photocopied or
hand-drawn road map
that depicts the route
of the trip

* Crayons or colored pencils

Before You Play

1. Make copies of road maps or
players can create hand-drawn
maps, leaving enough room to
add landmarks and other features
(an advantage of hand-drawn
maps).

2. Before you hand out the maps,
discuss the length of the route,
the distance, and approximately
how long the trip will take.

3. For older players, draw the maps to
scale and include a key or legend.

How To Play

1. Players observe and draw the
landmarks they pass: cities,
mountains, bridges, highways,
farms, animals, etc.

2. Players can use the maps to see
how much distance has been
covered and how much farther
they have yet to travel.

Travel Songfest

Age Group: 5-11
How Many Can Play: 2 or more
Objective: To learn new songs and have fun singing.

Materials

* Lyrics from favorite songs and songbooks, such as the *Girl Scout Pocket Songbook*

Before You Play

1. Invite girls to come prepared to sing their favorite songs and/or bring songs and CDs to share.

2. Prepare a list of songs to be sung in rounds.

How To Play

1. Start with songs that everyone knows (especially Girl Scout songs).

2. Encourage girls to teach the group new songs.

3. Sing along to the CDs that girls have brought.

4. For a large group, it is helpful to have a song leader. Encourage girls to take turns being the song leader.

Keep In Mind

Encourage girls to learn songs in languages other than English, including signing.

Variations

* Adapt or make up lyrics to popular songs. Choose winners for the silliest lyrics.

* Make up songs about sights while traveling: the landscape, the train ride, etc.

Girl Scouts together, that is our song.
Winding the old trails, rocky and long.
Learning our motto, living our creed.
Girl Scouts together, in every good deed

Girl Scouts together, happy are we.
Friendly to neighbors, far o'er the sea
Faithful to country, loyal to home.
Known as true Girl Scouts wherever we roam.

Traditional Games

Traditional games like hide-and-seek, hopscotch, and three-legged races are still popular. They offer children opportunities to engage in healthy indoor and outdoor play with little equipment. Encourage girls to talk to their parents/guardians and grandparents about the games they played when they were young.

Play traditional games:

* When there is a need for a filler between activities or the group needs a change of pace

* When two or more groups get together

* If girls are working on intergenerational activities

61

Duck, Duck, Goose

Age Group: 5-8

How Many Can Play: 6 or more

Objective: For the "goose" to catch "It" before she reaches the goose's seat.

Materials: None

How To Play

1. One player volunteers to be "It." The other players sit cross-legged in a large circle.

2. "It" walks around the outside of the circle, gently tapping each player on the head and saying "Duck!"

3. When "It" taps a player and yells, "Goose!" that player jumps up and chases "It" around the circle.

4. If "It" runs back to the "Goose's" spot in the circle without being tagged, the "Goose" becomes "It." If "It" is caught, the "Goose" returns to her place and "It" begins tapping players again.

Keep In Mind

Duck!

To avoid one player remaining "It" for too long, set a number of turns (maybe three or four) before another player becomes the new "It."

Hot Potato

Age Group: 5-11
How Many Can Play: 4 or more
Objective: To not get caught holding the "hot potato."

Materials

* An object to pass (tennis ball, beanbag, real potato, etc.)
* Timer
* CDs or music tapes and player (optional)

How To Play

1. Players sit cross-legged in a circle. Designate a game leader. The game leader sets the timer and puts the potato in play by gently tossing it to a player in the circle. (If tossing a potato, encourage players to use an underhand pass, as it is safer to catch.)

2. The potato is passed around the circle, or tossed from player to player, as quickly as possible. If the potato drops, the nearest player picks it up and puts it back into play.

3. When the timer sounds, the game leader calls "Hot Potato!" and play stops instantly.

4. The player holding the potato (or the last one to touch it if it is in the air) leaves the circle.

5. The game continues until one player is left in the circle. She is the winner.

Variation

Use music to signal the start and end of the game.

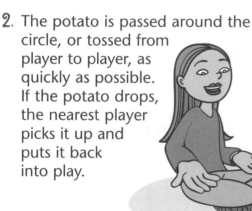

London Bridge

Age Group: 5-8
How Many Can Play: 5 or more
Objective: To avoid being caught while passing under the "bridge."

Materials

* Chalk or masking tape

Before You Play

1. Explain that this version of London Bridge ends with a game of tug-of-war.

2. Draw a line for the tug-of-war. If playing outdoors, use chalk; if indoors, mark with masking tape.

How To Play

1. Two players face each other on either side of the marked line and join hands. With arms raised high, they form an arch. These two players are the towers of the bridge. They secretly decide which one will be the gold tower and which will be silver.

2. The other players form a line on one side of the bridge. Each player takes a turn marching under the bridge, while everyone sings:

London Bridge is falling down,
Falling down, falling down,
London Bridge is falling down,
My dear lady.

3. On "My dear lady," the arch lowers, trapping the player within. That player is taken prisoner to the tower of her choice. She whispers either "silver" or "gold" to the two towers so no one else can hear, and then stands behind the tower she chose.

4. The game resumes with the other players passing under the bridge, while singing another stanza.

> *Take the key and lock her up,*
> *Lock her up, lock her up,*
> *Take the key and lock her up,*
> *My dear lady.*

The new prisoner whispers her choice of either the gold or silver tower.

5. The game continues with different stanzas sung (see stanzas below) until each prisoner is standing behind the tower of her choice.

6. When the last prisoner has been placed, the gold and silver teams line up behind their lead tower person for the tug-of-war. The sides may be unequal.

7. Each player clasps her hands around the waist of the player directly in front. The two original towers grasp each other's hands while standing behind the tug-of-war lines. On the count of three, the teams tug until one leader is pulled completely over the line. The other team is the winner.

Additional Stanzas

> *Build it up with iron bars,*
> *Iron bars, iron bars,*
> *Build it up with iron bars,*
> *My dear lady.*
>
> *Build it up with steel and stone,*
> *Steel and stone, steel and stone. . .*
>
> *Steel and stone will bend and break,*
> *Bend and break, bend and break. . .*

Variation

Sing the lyrics in a language other than English.

Jacks

Age Group: 8-11
How Many Can Play: 1 or more
Objective: To bounce the ball and pick up the correct number of jacks in sequence.

Materials

* Ball and 10 jacks (enough sets to accommodate teams)

How To Play

1. If the group is large, divide into teams of two to four girls. Players sit on the floor, clustered in their teams.

2. To decide who goes first, players balance a set of jacks on the back of their hands, lightly toss them in the air, and catch as many as possible. The player who catches the most jacks goes first.

3. Players begin each round by gently tossing the 10 jacks so that they spread out on the ground. If two (or more) jacks are touching, they are called "kisses" and the player has the option of picking up the kissing jacks and tossing them again.

4. The first round is called "onesies." The player throws the ball in the air, picks up one jack with her throwing hand, lets the ball bounce once, and catches the ball with the same hand.

(Beginners can be allowed two bounces.) The first jack is set aside. If the player does not pick up the correct number of jacks, drops the jacks, or fails to catch the ball, her turn is over.

5. Once a player successfully completes onesies, she immediately moves on to "twosies," and so on, until all 10 jacks have been retrieved.

6. It usually takes several turns to complete each round. The first player to make it through tensies wins.

Variation

Eggs in a Basket

Player begins by gently throwing the jacks on the ground. If the right hand is used to toss the ball, the left hand rests on the ground with the palm up to make a "basket." Player tosses the ball, picks up the jack(s) with her right hand and quickly transfers them to her left hand, the "basket," and catches the ball after one bounce. Players start at onesies. The first to complete tensies is the winner.

Simon Says

Age Group: 5–11
How Many Can Play: 4 or more
Objective: To follow Simon's instructions and be the last player standing.

Materials: None

How To Play

1. One player is designated as Simon.

2. Simon faces the players who are lined up side-by-side at arms-length distance.

3. Simon gives the orders while demonstrating the task. Players obey the orders only when Simon prefaces the instructions with the words "Simon Says." For example, "Simon says, 'Hands on head.'" Players mimic Simon and put their hands on their head.

4. If Simon omits the words "Simon Says" and players follow the order, they are out of the game.

5. The winner is the last player standing.

Simon says put your hands in the air!

Mother, May I?

Age Group: 5-8
How Many Can Play: 3 or more
Objective: To be the first player to reach "Mother."

Materials

✳ Chalk or masking tape

Mother may I?

Before You Play

Mark start and finish lines about 25 feet apart.

How To Play

1. The player chosen as "Mother" stands at the finish line, facing the other players who are lined up on the starting line.

2. Each player takes turns asking Mother for permission to move forward. The first player might ask, "Mother, may I take three giant steps?"

3. Mother can respond however she wants. She could answer, "No, but you may take 10 baby steps," or she could say, "Yes, you may take three giant steps." If the player receives a "Yes" answer, she must still ask, "Mother, may I?" If Mother says, "Yes, you may," the player moves forward as directed. If Mother changes her mind and says, "No, you may not," the player cannot move.

4. If the player forgets to ask permission to move forward or makes the wrong move, she goes back to the starting line.

The game continues until one player (Mother's "favorite") crosses the finish line and is declared the winner. This player could become Mother in the next round.

Red Light, Green Light

Age Group: 5-11
How Many Can Play: 3 or more
Objective: To be the first player to reach the "light."

Materials

✳ Chalk or masking tape

Before You Play

Mark start and finish lines about 25 feet apart.

How To Play

1. Designate a player to be the "light." The light stands at the finish line with her back to the others, who are lined up on the starting line.

2. Whenever the light calls out "Green light!" the other players move forward as fast as they can.

3. Players must freeze whenever the light suddenly turns and calls "Red light!" Any players caught moving are sent back to the starting line.

4. The light turns back around and play resumes.

5. The first player to tag the light is the winner and becomes the next light.

Green light!

Three-Legged Race

Age Group: 8-11
How Many Can Play: 4 or more
Objective: To be the first pair to cross the finish line.

Materials

* Large bandana for each pair of girls
* Chalk or masking tape

Before You Play

Mark start and finish lines about 50 feet apart.

How To Play

1. Each player finds a partner. It is best if partners are close in height.

2. Designate a "caller" who will also tie the bandanas for the partners.

3. Partners stand side-by-side, with arms around each other's waists. The caller will tie their inside legs together loosely at the ankles with a bandana. This creates their "third" leg.

4. On "Go!" the pairs run toward the finish line.

5. The first pair to cross the finish line wins.

Keep In Mind

It is best to play this game on a soft surface, like grass.

Variation

If the group is large, divide into even teams and run a relay race.

Jump Rope Rhymes

Age Group: **8-11**
How Many Can Play: **3 or more**
Objective: To recite rhymes while establishing a jumping rhythm.

Materials

* Jump rope or heavy clothesline (14-16 feet in length for every 4-6 players or 10-12 feet in length for every two players)

Before You Play

Tie a knot at each end of the clothesline for handles.
Explain that it is up to the rope-turners to make smooth, rhythmic turns.

How To Play

1. Two players turn the rope while the other players take turns jumping in and out while reciting the rhymes.

2. The sound of the rope touching the ground is the signal to jump in.

3. Jumpers should move quickly into the rope, without touching it. They should jump upright, with arms held straight down, or with elbows bent, or with elbows bent and hands clasped at the stomach, looking straight ahead.

Sample Jump Rope Rhymes:

Mabel, Mabel

Mabel, Mabel, set the table,
Just as fast as you are able!
Put on plates, forks, salt,...etc.
And don't forget the RED HOT PEPPER!
(Rope-turners turn rope as fast as possible.)

Apples, Peaches, Pears, and Plums

Apples, peaches, pears, and plums
Tell me when your birthday comes.
January, February, March,...etc.

Miss Mary Mack

Miss Mary Mack, Mack, Mack,
All dressed in black, black, black,
With silver buttons, buttons, buttons,
All down her back, back, back.

She asked her mother, mother, mother,
For fifty cents, cents, cents,
To see the elephants, elephants, elephants,
Jump the fence, fence, fence.

They jumped so high, high, high,
They touched the sky, sky, sky,
And didn't come back, back, back,
Till the fourth of July, July, July!

Teddy Bear

Teddy bear, teddy bear,
Turn around.
Teddy bear, teddy bear,
Touch the ground.
Teddy bear, teddy bear,
Show your shoe.
Teddy bear, teddy bear,
That will do!
Teddy bear, teddy bear,
Go upstairs.
Teddy bear, teddy bear,
Say your prayers.
Teddy bear, teddy bear,
Switch off the light.
Teddy bear, teddy bear,
Say, "Good night!"

Spanish Jump Rope Rhymes:

Arbolito de Peru
(Little Tree From Perú)

A (ah)...(E) eh...I (ee)...
O (oh)...U (ooo)

Arbolito de Peru
(Little tree from Perú)

Dime cuantos años tienes tú?
(Tell me how old are you?)

Uno, dos, tres, cuatro, cinco, seis, siete,
ocho, nueve, diez, once, doce...
(One, two, three, four, five, six, seven,
eight, nine, ten, eleven, twelve,...)

Uno, Dos, Tres
(One, Two, Three)

Uno, dos, tres—Cho
Uno, dos, tres—co
Uno, dos, tres—la
Uno, dos, tres—te
Bate, bate Cho-co-la-te!
(Beat, beat, chocolate!)

String Games

Age Group: 6-11
How Many Can Play: 1 or more
Objective: To create "structures" from string.

Materials

✳ Approximately 2 feet of string or thin yarn

Before You Play

Tie the ends of the string or yarn together.

How To Play

Players weave the string evenly through their thumbs, index, middle, ring, and little fingers. The strands of string nearest the body are called the "near strings." Strands or loops farthest from the body are called the "far strings." A string in front of the palm is called a "palmar string."

Fish Spear

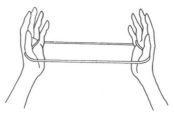

Beginning position: hold the hands so that palms face each other. Hook the string around both thumbs first. Then hook the little fingers under the string so that the string rests across the palms.

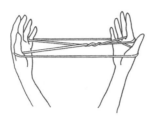

1. The right index finger picks up the left palmar string from underneath. While moving the hands apart, turn the index finger to twist the loop a few times.

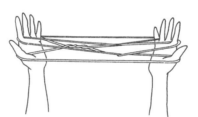

2. The left index finger, picks up the string crossing the right palm by reaching through the right index loop.

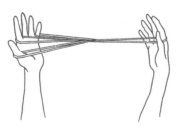

3. Move the hands apart and release the right thumb and little finger of the right hand. This is the "fishing spear!" The right index finger holds the handle of the spear. The left thumb, index, and little finger hold the points.

Cat's Whiskers

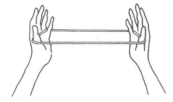

Beginning position: hold the hands so that palms face each other. Hook the string around both thumbs first. Then hook the little fingers under the string so that the string rests across the palms.

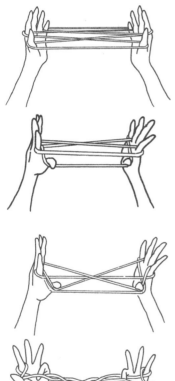

1. The right index finger goes under the left palmar string. Spread the fingers and pull the string back. Do the same with the other hand. This is the "Cat's cradle."

2. The string is freed from both thumbs. The far little finger string is picked up on the backs of the thumbs by reaching under with both thumbs. The thumbs then go back to their original position.

3. Place the thumbs over the near index strings. Pick up the far index strings on the backs of the thumbs.

4. Free the little fingers. Place the little fingers over the closest strings. Then pick up the next string on the backs of the little fingers, which go back to their original position.

5. Release the thumbs. "Cat's whiskers" are formed!

Index

A

Active Games, 15–26

ages of players
 5–8 years, 16, 19, 23, 24,
  25, 29, 62, 64, 68
 5–11 years, 7, 8, 9, 11,
  12, 18, 20, 22, 28, 31,
  32, 34, 48, 52, 53,
  57, 59, 60, 63, 67, 69
 6–11 years, 6, 10, 13, 17,
  21, 30, 33, 35, 38, 39,
  40, 44, 45, 49, 54, 55,
  56, 58, 74
 8–11 years, 36, 46, 47,
  66, 70, 71

Alphabet, 38

Alphabet Search, 52

Alphabet Story, 39

¡Alto! (un juego de Méjico),
 42–43

Animal, Vegetable, Mineral,
 58

awards, games to play
 when working for, 15

B

Balloon Relay, 17

Beanbag Bull's Eye, 20

Book Worm, 31

Bubble Fun, 8

Buzz, 44

C

Car and Driver, 29

Caterpillar Race, 30

Cat's Cradle, 76

Cat's Whiskers, 76

Centipedes, 7

change of pace, games to
 play for, 15, 61

Chase the Tail, 28

Circle Ball, 16

Cliffhanger, 53

cliquishness, games for
 minimizing, 27

D

Define It!, 47

disabilities, games for girls
 with, 4

Duck, Duck, Goose, 62

E

Eggs in a Basket, 66

F

Fish Spear, 75

fitness, games to play for,
 15

free play, games for, 61

G

games, value of, to girls'
 development, 4

Girl Scout Hopscotch,
 25–26

Girl Scout songs, 60

Go, Car, Go!, 19

Grab Bag, 18

group dynamic, games for
 strengthening, 27

groups getting together
 games to play at
  ceremonies, 5
 games to play, 61

H

healthy living,
 games for, 15

Hopscotch Relay, 23

Hot Potato, 63

Human Spelling Bee, 32

I

I'm Thinking Of . . . 58

intergenerational activities,
 games to play during, 61

Notes

# Notes